P9-EDE-662

THE WEATHER BOOK

THE WEATHER BOOK

Janet Kauffman

The Weather Book, by Janet Kauffman, is published in cooperation with the
Associated Writing Programs and is an *AWP Award Series Selection*.

ISBN 0-89672-089-6 (paper)
ISBN 0-89672-090-X (cloth)
Library of Congress Catalog Card Number: 81-50883
Designed by Betty M. Johnson, set in Highland,
printed on Texas Tech Opaque, 70 lb.
Cover and dust jacket design based on photograph by Sigrid Carter
Texas Tech Press, Lubbock, Texas 79409
Copyright 1981 by Texas Tech University
Printed in the United States of America

Acknowledgments

Permission from the following to reprint the poems listed is gratefully acknowledged.

Ark River Review: "Change & No Change"
Axletree: "Neanderthal"
Beloit Poetry Journal: "Mennonite Farm Wife"
Chicago Review: "Penelope Unwinding," Vol. 28, No. 3, copyright 1977
Mississippi Review: "Postcard: Match," "Driving"
The Nation: "Off-Loom Weaving"
The Ohio Journal: "Rally"
Poetry Now: "Summer," "Appetizer, for You," "The Fall of Leaves," "Grapes," "The End of March," "Fall Plowing," "Guerilla" from "Hitching the Americas"
A Change in Weather, edited by Peg Lauber, Eau Claire, Wisconsin: Rhiannon Press, 1978: "Swamp" from "Muckland Farms"
The Third Coast, edited by Herbert Scott, Conrad Hilberry, and James Tipton, Detroit: Wayne State University Press, 1976: "Topping, As Preface," "Steamer on the Seedbed," "Cultivating," "Taking Down" from "Working Tobacco," "Watercress," "The Volunteers"
Wind: "The Womb in the World"

CONTENTS

III   RALLY

I   MATCH

Beginning of the Book

The first winter here without wood
I chewed my cheek, shaping hollows,
starving myself like a poor soul
pitched under willows on a prairie.

That was a time for scraping the womb
clean, for combing hair, bathing,
and walking the toppled fields in cold
lively winds, snow thrashing among weeds.

The middle of November (I made a note)
I cooked you up. I'd write you into spring,
a neighbor, farther than Nebraska,
who lived quietly, with a certain pallor

and a mind made up: you said I was alive.
I was. That was the beginning, you recall,
of the unraveling. It's years
since you came, compassionless,

set up the room where you write to me,
stored bags for your travel.
At first it was not out of love
I wrote, I thought; but at last

I'm sending the book of weathers
charted through winters. I still keep track.
Did you get my last card showing white mules and hay?
The message *au verso*: Full moon. No rain.

Postcard: Match

Alfred, you're a sweet child but I live with mother
and know too much. I don't like your walk.
You won't look me in the mouth. We're no match.
Send your one-eyed brother over, though—
the sullen one. I'll try to teach him
a few phrases, even if no one else would
care to see him speak: imagine
the animated, grinding chin,
slow, unhinged, and the one eye
driven into focus—he'd see me.
Think what he might tell of all he knows
of sixteen years in quiet from the time
lightning struck the pine tree and it burned
they said in blue flames as it fell.

Summer

I ate green peaches, pretending they were hatched
jungle fruits, the rare ones women find
under wide slick leaves lifted back like sheets,
the fruit right there, uncovered fresh,
dull with fuzz, bedborn overnight.
I ate them like grenades thinking this will do the trick.
I'll lie here green and wait until I puff up, float
inside where I will hold to a straight-backed chair
and whisper: send me somewhere empty, unripe.

Mennonite Farm Wife

She hung her laundry in the morning
before light and often in winter
by sunrise the sheets were ice.
They swung all day on the line,
creaking, never a flutter.
At dusk I'd watch her lift each one
like a field, the stretches of white
she carried easily as dream
to the house where she bent and folded
and stacked the flat squares.
I never doubted they thawed
perfectly dry, crisp,
the corners like thorn.

First Words

First words can hardly be our own:
replies to a gunman
fool like someone else's
instinct—I don't have a thing
you want. Nothing.
We die. Or go on living.

Even in the commonplace
simplicities of love,
barring risk or risking,
either way, the unknowing
phrases of belief match crime's
chances. We say only what we can.

The Womb in the World

Roto-tilled like an ancient crusty garden,
white-rooted clumps of witch grass
kicked up, nerves
tangled through huge red clots;
an inhuman territory, unearthed.
No place for worms or feeling
one's way; no place for seeds,
infiltrators, redeemers.
Meet me, machine—
tiller, attuner, that we might engender
anomaly: the steel leek,
mechanized berries (wired
to cluster), aromatic pipewrenches,
the interchangeable root.

Change & No Change

Winds lift the frogs out of the high swamp,
fly them over the house, their legs dangling,
their green throat chorus wheeling in sirens.

I'm struggling with it again—
the allure of catastrophe and its tricks:
winding scarves, sudden doves.

I feel the bony hands around my ribs,
a father tossing a child, hallooing here I am,
laughing as I fly, I'm here, all's well,
there is no change, I fall, there is no change,

even if winds scatter Texas sheep in the grass,
and the trees all rise in flame.

Two, At Odds

1

The nights of no moon you drive in
from town, from trees, from wind
to move like a room around me.
You, like the lid of an eye,
are my dark, my blind.

2

I sit in the sun alone,
a book warm on my thighs.
You have been gone for days.
These are the long afternoons
of sparrows, seed, song—
ordinary promise and full sun.
Across the field in a line
are five horses and five men
and a steady forwardness
into the breeze. A green cap
spins off, a rider circles.
The eddies of the afternoon
alter, all things shift,
leaves twist and the sun now
gives free rein. Get up.
Get going. Get on home.

Working Tobacco

1   Topping, As Preface

We soaped our hands
with cold soap from a tin can,
then slipped into the rows.
We pulled tobacco suckers, snapped them down,
broke off the pastel flowering tops, with slick fingers
feeling over each plant,
parting the green gumleaves,
steady as prophets who knew how to do things
effortlessly, hands taking charge,
blessing and breaking,
blessing, breaking.

2   Steamer on the Seedbed

Machines
like mothers pumping the beginning
every April on schedule,
spring steamed
out from under iron,
the metal lids lifting—
and there it was:
great gates opening,
whirring gears and camshafts
winging, the ungainly steamer
shaking wide bull flanks,
shimmering
heatwaves rising through unsteady air,
white clouds bursting into blue
and in the breeze the stinging
water spat off iron.

Somewhere inside the steamer's belly
roared fire.

3   Cultivating

On a two-seated cultivator, we sniffed exhaust,
inhaled blue clouds those long rose evenings;
leaning on a handle in each hand
we weaved around the stalks, furrowing
damp field into dark.
Doubled over and in the drug of it
I watched the velvet plants
with hair leaves moving untouched
below the tractor body, between harrows,
drifting like the blessed on their way.
I let them go.

> *Tobacco's but an Indian weed,*
> *Grows green in the Morn, cut down at Eve...*

And now when I see in the shadow of porches
grey farm women nodding
at grey slippered feet,
I feel all over again the curve in my back,
the disproportionate torso
turned like a shell,
the vaginal hold on empty space
and that blue monoxide
cloud of summer we bent beneath to breathe.

4   Leaf

Leaf upon leaf
embroidered on a forest,
gold leaf from green
rib and mesh, elaborate
wind-lifting flags and Caesar's laurels,
miniaturized
forget-me-not leaves in margins,
leave-taking,
palms, pines

simplified to lines—

we draw these
first, a scrawl,
a sign for sure.

5 Cutting

The tall frame wagons were a rocking
scaffolding on iron wheels.
Tobacco hung like dollar bills,
long and losing green, the thicknesses
of leaf and stalk, gum-hair
plants to lean against, full-length.
In the shed it was the dark hand to hand
swing—catch—swing—catch—
hook of tobacco hanging:
uncle on the rafters overhead,
grandpa over him, straddling air,
father in the black peaked top.
A brown and bitter dust fell down.
The wagons empty, outside,
our cheeks sucked in—it's good—
tasting the grit, the clear
vinegar punch in August in the dry field.

6 Vinegar Punch

Is vinegar and water,
simple to remember as Jesus wept,
with no more sugar than you must,
and nutmeg
you filter through teeth,
sweep with the tongue, spit.

7   Song for Harmonica

Sir Walter Raleigh is a bust,
a pleasant face upon a sac:

in velvet and opaque pearls
he is a man the girls will say

they lust—they may—knowing well
he's occupied with plots, polite

assassinations, speculative
deals—he's shaking Red Man

hands and taking home the green
leaves, in the hold at sea

curing gold. Who should tell
the story of a pleasant man

with money, paying what he will
for pleasure, and the ruddy girls

and fathers farming for his leisure?

8   Taking Down

A swinging trouble light sweeps through black
barn and cold. My father's breath the fog overhead
caught like a bush in the cone of low beam.
He walks on rails, November nights,
handing down tobacco, long leaves
flattened by the hang and like skins
stretched, veins dry.
We move mechanically under
huge roofed spaces,
among the hammered edges of machines—
tractors, harrows, plows hauled in,
the planter and the flatbed wagons.

Not hunters,
not driven,
we work and do without
the power to cast the shadow of iron,
even as the stun, the hush of arrow over snow—
that speeding dark—comes home.

Neanderthal

The hand has everything to do
with rock. Hand and rock
hammer, and the rock shapes hand.
Fist is rock, palm is
rock-hollowed for holding
rock, even the bones
of fingers curve in rest,
welcoming neither handshake
nor caress of buttock, breast,
without the longing for what
will not give.
Even skin and fold recall
silica, granite, the sheen
of serpentine,
and not clay.

Postcard: Unavailing

I have a poem,
medieval, cadaverous,
in another typewriter—let blood
thickening, voices tumultuous and God-assailing.
It's a dream.

You in another place
move about a floored room with walls
in wood, in thought. You play
handball, I hear, too, and but for your breathing,
there's calm.

Between us, this

weather,
the lidded houses,
highways,
and the mines.

Orchards, fields,
these lines.

Watercress

It was cold, and we gritted our teeth,
hands hooking under, cutting blind
in the black spring just out from rock.
Rooted to water, the tangle of green
we reached almost out of our reach
and carried back kettles of cress,
back through the orchard, the subdivision—
awkward, lucky as cooks
side-stepping soldiers, the slumped regiments—
with leaves pressing flat to our tongues
and a taste no remedy (no, not blood),
but the bite of a breaking
spring, its cold flows.

Grapes

My mother did not like grapevines
or grapes, not even the blue ones
with large seeds growing lustrous
and swinging overhead like lamps
in her mother's arbor—there were wasps
on the first ones ripening,
drinking at all the ones fallen—
although her mother still talks of the press
underfoot as she walked there
the hottest days she says
in the cool, the stir.

Muckland Farms

1 Shady Water

Up against the shady water
wall of settled swamp:
this is the end of the road.
I knew it hanging back,
the deep here like the shallow,
imperturbable. This could be a way
through horror, the hallowed
swallowing I won't go into—
the coal and damp and bones
maybe mine, what home I have.

2 Hook

Lenny Moore with his hook right hand
worked a backhoe, laid pipe
for fifteen acres of black peat
straight down thirty feet. He says
he thinks he'll grow potatoes
round as washed rocks. With any luck
he says he'll pick among his honeydews
the half-moon claw of a thing
that looked as you'd expect
for a firm hold at the swamp edge.

3   *Orchis spectabilis*

Where but in unluxurious lower Michigan,
where but a temperate county
with crops from anhydrous ammonia, and M&S
Manufacturing, Inc., where else
would a jungle flower of six
small mouths open to tongue
fern and sharp grasses, under golden
bellwort and fringed waterleaf
by the water in the woods, where else
would this flower and succulent
stalk suggest geological change,
or turn in the sun historical
as a Russian coin in the garden
or ancient bone child in the field?

4   Swamp

The revving out of turns
at Cambridge Junction Speedway is the thunder
through dusk. Jets trail still in the sun,
slowing for Detroit and the blue
line of lights at Metro. Not far away
here is swamp: a heron,
great blue, at the edge, unmoving.
We lean against the car and talk
when suddenly the heron
chokes out a long *all, all is lost.*
We see a rise of neck
as if the neck would lift the rest,
and then the wings work
mechanically. The neck folds.
There is no way to call
heron, heron, my shoulder
would hold you. For you
I would not breathe.

II HITCHING THE AMERICAS

1

Crossed over swimming, one
into another, in slow currents taken
the length of the river ledge.
Washed, silted
sand along skin, a continent's
streams gone measureless.
I found a warmer side,
low, easy with shallows and hatching curls,
rocks, too, like eggs uncharmed,
unmatched.

2

And there was the butcher's truck
first thing,

picked me up. I rode the beginning
turns in a dark
flow of the lamb's sides,

rocked with the cold
thighs and held firm
fingers around the hook
through the dread strung tendon like my own
heel, or neck unnerved.

I look out two stained windows of the truck.
The road lifts away
umbilical
through new, washed space.

We're headed to market at Techitla.

3

Here are houses
and women out of houses.
As if with a blessing their arms
move through the ancient configurations.
Innumerable arms.

—roll it out the hard ground
no it is not right the first one—

and she takes it all
the circle
stuffed in hand she eats it
hides it fast still raw inside.

4

The birth
south and rugged, into a body
I could only think I had moved this time
out of the mind. Am I hanging
by the hamstring? Sensing
the lost head, hair that should twine?
Or is this the animal
tracking downwind, head up?—
a first sharp breath,
arms, legs, untried
blue swimming feet only now reaching air, now cloth.

All right. Get out.
Which way you going?

5

I bought a silver ring from a child
at the first awning.

Caught a ride with a Swiss dealer
in diamonds, in his black Continental
rental. Mexico. C'est une merveille.
C'est le soleil. He said that twice,

and he talked to me as I slept.

6

The milk of breathing here
the feast
of breast and fullness
through flower

jungle jungle jungle

Mother I've lost my way,
which is which?—
Child, do you miss me too?

I hadn't expected to travel
rivers and places of no decay.
The soft molds root.

Paths of matted leaf, mother,
heave like lungs
and the cold if it comes
falls in threads of rain.

Pink wax petals,
childleaves,
and the yellow velvet blossoms, little one,
reach through the crowded stalks
to feed.

Night does not sleep,
does not darken. The banquet embraces—
more, more
drink, let us drink.

7   Story

For lunch yesterday,
met my father's cousin's son
with the Mennonite Volunteer Service
in Tegucigalpa.
We ate bread he brought and fruit.

"Disaster's no holiday!" He was laughing,
recalling Hazel up the coast, Diane
along the Gulf, and the one that brought him here,
breaking palms and washing through Trujillo.

Honduras. He'd brought a few things,
stayed through the war, and stayed on,
a kid driving jeep inland and places
he'd never dreamed. He said he never dreamed

before Honduras. Now at night
large trees thrust up from his shoulders,
root through his arms and feed
"as if I were loam and sand and rock."

He's been writing a story
about a Mennonite boy who goes to war
unlike his family who live in the dry and clear of autumn
grains, and gardens
held over winter in hot beds, in the radiant
mists of a greenhouse, tomatoes
for Christmas.

The child leaves the luxuriant
fields and briar
underbrush of a child's woods.

"I cannot keep these things to myself."

Running away, he finds an amber bottle
under leaves in the mud by a stream,
the bottle broken, and heaped inside

spiraled shells. "The sea only recently
slipped hundreds of miles away."

As he crosses a border he is thinking
about the severely worn
hair of the peaceful women,
and the family's laughing men
in the shade of summer reunions:
they wear ironed shirts and lean back;
they cross their legs at the ankles;
they watch children slide the stainless steel slide.
They have what they had.

"Some people I will not let die."

Rescue
for the boy is war, increasing risk
of knowing that goodness could not have been
"where it appeared
always to hold my life."

We'd never met before. At two we said goodbye
hurriedly, shaking hands. I sat a long while
where I was when he had gone.

Last night I dreamed his Mennonite boy,
tall, limber as a palm,
brought me the amber bottle
and the shells, and did not mention war
or his wounds, or his new life.

8   Cadaver

Not one city
through to Peru. In the highlands
this one out of the past, unpaved.
I came here on a cart wide with baskets
and the driver's cousins claiming
cousins in doorways

until at a turn the city quiets
strangely.
Time has nothing to do with it.

Bright houses age,
grow steeply gabled.
The white light narrows
as brown clouds like waters of lakes
gather without shadow.

The city we see to our disbelief
emptied—war, disease,
no telling. No this is not the place!
the family cries, several of them
where?
gone from the cart as it veers
sharply. We reach and we reach for them,
catch them back, afraid for the sickness
they have brushed with—
yes they are bruised,
their shoulders, ah their cheeks.

A policeman
at an intersection—someone!—
pushes with angry arms
away, away
as if the mule, our small slow cart
here where there is nothing
blocked the life of a place.

Obedient, the mule heads off
through more leaden air.
The street widens
and now we can see the distant blue
mountain rising. —We can go,
the driver talks like a dreamer.

But, in the middle of the street
with the mountain still
blue and absolute, far ahead

we see two men
one flat to the ground, the other over him

beating, beating,
no
he does not miss
no
and closer, we see the man on the ground

is dead, a bullethole and a compass turn of blood
on a cloth coat. It is a policemen who beats him,
thrashes furious as a lover over the dead
beloved, the body unrenderable.
With the bludgeoning now, the policeman
has torn through flesh and as if by design
opens the abdomen, exposes liver, bowels dazzling,
and he pitches the heavy nightstick,
and he pulls by handfuls now, throws it all upon the dust street,
the still firm and splendidly scarlet
globes of the whole man.

When I saw in the past
two blue children lifted by daylight
into opening childspaces,
I thought then of death
and of death and of death
again with new things.

Here I said: pulses and warm ones
you live and the dust springs with you.
Here is a warmth not weatherly,
and cadaver you sing.

9 Guerilla

Small and careening, slavish
insects accompany me
around my eyes, diving
deep into my hair.

After weeks of fighting
through the air of them,
my face is swollen, unseemly,
and still they whirl
resolute, fine-winged.

Sniper fire is nothing to this.
I no longer sleep.
Out of the valleys to the east at night
flares a constant fire, and within the city
curtained limousines deliver the handcuffed
women to places they will not live through.

I write in the dark to my lovers
and do not move as incoming rounds
reach the house. My four sweet
lovers like furnished rooms
in a countryside of woods and farms
are warm. Are they warm?

I write them a few lines a week
and say I have met an official
who may help, or a child
who yesterday took my hand
and showed me a fine bronze statue in the park.

III   RALLY

Postcard: The Hill

I want to show you a hill
that shifts with winds,
only the flecked rocks holding
fields as farm.

But it's winter, and under snow
the hill moves itself
into dreamslope, remote,
lost as Nepal.

You know what I'm saying.
The hill that drifts to a stream

must be the stretch of your arm in sleep,
or mine, which I have never seen.

Penelope Unwinding

By design each morning
I have got nowhere.
With the rhythmic shuttling of silken
threads into another father's shroud—
this is my own
detouring—back and forth
each night, I grow younger,
as if hand over hand I descended
from clouded disorderly kingdoms
where I had no voice and was aging
before the polished eyes of infants.
It is my undoing
gains me time:
fathers do not die,
husbands continue lost,
suitors pour more drinks, complain, prop their feet—
and I am myself, unchanged.

Only when I am
found out, my son, will you see
it was not as you thought,
this marking time.

The enormous lengths of
nothingness I have woven
worked me whole
and fully I have opened myself to events.
I have made and unmade a dozen
fine robes, the folds of this room have
held you—see how I hold you.
Invisibly we pull
home steadily the lost
father, husband, and the love,

love we will have back
within our rooms. Telemachus,

oh we are favored
with time. Have even the gods
in their monotony worked this way,
lovingly, simply
for a return,
for a house—I will not see the blood
you will see—through love at last
cleared.

The Fall of Leaves

Shade Gap is a mountain town of thinning men
and scarab-eyed teenagers leaning at doors
like the sour fogs of the slopes.
The town has suffered three years
an infestation of oaks. Behind the high school
Shade Mountain lets fall its brown leaves,
each one whole, clean to the ribs, all lace.

People say, Imagine
clothes of these leaves.

Others say, It is marvelous,
the disguise of disease.

Or they say, I dream
leaves, and loose muslins,
nets, and veils.

They do not seek a cure; they attend
their season of awe and await the astonishing
thoroughness none would have credited,
the destruction they would not have predicted
could change their minds.

Ice Storm

Clearing eyes see simply
ice and the wonder
is each one, each one separately
knows vision a saint claims
must begin like this,

the sun prismatic and absolute,
a polar day for saying no or yes.

No, ice has no will of its own.
Yes, it is pure and dangerous.
Yes, ice is like the eye.

I had forgot what the world was like.
This is not the customary
muddle of insects and breezes.
How will I remember these breakables,
lavish on lilacs, when the lilacs bud?

Today, six boys lie twisted in the road.
Today the fox leaves no track in the snow.

Camp on the Monkiel Glacier

Boulders from a caving
mouth of ice
here rock each other over miles,
miles of a past
left to pass. Only the dead
grey eggs of the dead know these fields
where we sleep.

      Nothing moves.
      Nothing lives here, although once

at night we wake to a scrambling
spill of rock
high above. We hear it cascading
downslope, the staggering roll
nearer, and then an unbreathing
dark closes.

      We stretch again long-legged
      in the sprawl of dream
      through lengths of night seas rocking their harbors
      where small flashing fish

live by fear,
and by camouflage
sway among grasses, turn
between crusted rocks to their prey, the mouthfuls
of smaller whole bodies, perfectly
unaware they have disappeared into another.

Denial

Beginning the Fourth, July grows its claw
catalpa pods, blunt
hand-hammered nails.

By Bastille Day, catalpa beans
curve, they can sever
the thick horizon at dusk.

Tall houses circled with trees
feel the rattled air, needling.

Lovers warn: whatever happens
it is not true. The profusion
of mouths, teeth, tongues of tasting—
forget, wait, think of nothing.

July slows through the 31st.
The weather warms predictably.
No one talks in the shadows after dark.

Catalpa beans lengthen, halt in mid-air
as green velveted swords.

Blame the trees, blame them.

Fall Plowing

Crusted baguette
furrows—one, another
and another rolling east,
west on return.
When I was a child it was possible
to labor in crossing a field
against the iridescent
twists of clay.
I believed those polished folds
a farmer's doing, or plow's,
not then judging soil as laden,
luxuriant, yeasty,
feisty, glutinous,
umbrous, precious
amber loaf.

Catalpas

After a short season, flowering
late in June, filling
stringed seeds,
now this sudden brown collapse.

Children in the house
feel a trembling in the ear, from its hollows
where carved ivory
hammers ping in an autumn
interior.

Raked into heaps, ashy
veins splinter,
the huge heart of the leaf
in ruins. And so we begin
again, again.

Milkweed

Recall an autumn
scan of eyes, explosive light,
and the repercussive seeding
gift upon gift,
air lifting gift, again gift.

In January, riddled
with mottled brown pods,
sacs, absence,
abeyance,
even birds cannot see
thorned lacquered seeds by each rock.

Cat eyes, low
among discrepancies of stalk,
spine, heaped grasses,
an immense cover of sky—
barn cat
crouches in milkweed, her colors
flat, ditched, deadweed.
She blinks.

At the edge of the field,
barbed wire shrills
and the dissonant, laden
winds stir once more
milkweed, maracan.

The Volunteers

In the middle of the afternoon when people turn slowly
and never mind the smoke winds rolling,
the barn shingles snapped off all at once in flames.

The lid gone, everything flew out—hurrahs of fire
rocked the trees, and a small sun cooled.
The timbers of the peak bloomed full,

fell; and in the slow of dreamers watching
we saw a wheat field stretching out beyond,
a brushy line of woods, more sky.

—Well, that's your barndance—easy enough
now to have a party with the volunteers,

their numbered hats, their slick coats heaped on grass.
They were young, excited by the whole thing

done with, the drifting smoke, the hay and metal stink.
They drank Crush and 7-Up and smiled.

Under the trees they spread their legs
and leaned on elbows, each one seeing the same

flame gone, water spent, and the sun
fired up again, wind in curl.

The Green Combine

When you drive by in your green combine
on its toy wheels and lifted V
cornhead, I hear you turn
at the driveway, slow like a plane gearing down,
the engines dying, coasting
until you're stopped at the porch.

And there you are with your headphones around your neck,
in the living room just like a brother
lost for years in abandoned mines
in Idaho, and smiling
I came back.

We talk prices per bushel
and futures, the inexhaustible
statistics like kisses,
codes of the hybrids, Pioneer 412 C,
X-249, and the yields.

Outside the combine catches the rain; its bin fills.
The cab like a sacred place thrums with birds.
The green
rusts although vines from the side of the house
find their way there and wreathe
the choppers, the lengths of rollered belts,
battery, gears, the heart.

In your fields the corn lies down.
Deer, the escaped steers and cows
come there to feed.

What next? say the neighbors. They leap the porch railing,
to talk of neglect
and the things around here gone wild,
gone to seed.

Off-Loom Weaving

Ideally you would not be bothered by flies
but could sit in one spot,
handspun yarns at hand, at ease,
with this order allowing the random
development of, let's say,
organic constructions.
I sat however under our only tree
where fallen apples hummed
with crusty insects wandering into sweetness,
unpremeditated, pure.
I waved away what I could, and worked
the shed of the warp like a maw—it opened,
closed those days with the grim intent
of shark. The work was a meal
you may hang like a skin.

The Weaver on Weaving: Honeysuckle Pattern

How do you take a thing that is all sweet
aroma and make it a saleable item,
durable, in two-color combinations?—
an enterprising weaver asked with some interest
one cloudy Colonial day and worried over one clouded week
until out of her penciled drafts like roots
the numbered variations and linear turns suggested
not only bud, stalk, and leaf
but flower and round fruit filling
repeatedly. —And what is the sweetness
of honeysuckle, she said at last like a parson,
—but hot promises of sweet pickings?

Weeks later,
wrapping an indigo and white linen runner
—I find such satisfaction,
she commented to the buyer,
—in an idea's bout with form.
Whereupon the day bloomed, she thought,
as if it were Sunday and she'd lied.

Construction

You say that I should join
your crew—they're tanned, they chew,
they spit—
and I should quit dissembling,

begin assembling with you
a house that as we all agree is nothing but a box.

Here I've been clearing the shelves and tossing to Goodwill
my how-to books,
guides to Provence, the unalterable
grey Collected Cooper.

I'm done with brooming
cobwebs and lint from the roof of my mouth.
May I skid one last time in my socks
across the unobstructed hardwood floors?

I doubt I'd have used the hammer at home:
in the end I would not have wanted to de-frame
the living room windows or de-glaze the panes
or stack the glass squares for later
sledgehammering. I think not.
I've been warned before
about the teeth of saws.

Besides, I have already learned
how the builders tip to each other thick sheets of plywood,
how they balance along their wrists
2 × 4's stamped pink and graded fresh
for a 3-bedroom house pinescent.

Everything fits—
the fourteen rising steps of stairs,
the insulation in foil cocoons.
You too have noticed
cardboard buckets for nails look nothing like milk pails.

Oh where have gone the skirts of a ladling wind?

In damp concrete
windowless basements
more workmen plug into grounded grey sockets
their circular saws. They snap on black-corded trouble lights:
see the blades smile now,
the lumber on edge. Whizz—there's the leg of a table.
Bizzit—the arm of a chair.

Amoretti

The Rubens baby does have wings,
is sweet, bathed, reaching
featherlike for comfort motherflesh:
two buoyant bodies of a jeweled world

smiling and holding a globe for joy.
They play in curtained space,
the dark plush encompassing
cherubs, child, husband,

father, the somewhat cooler older
brother, without a shadow of
substance or presence.
Salvation's in pudding, they say,

they all say, and consequently the men
try always to hold two breasts at once.
The humming women spoonfeed daughters,
smile at slimming sons, rock them

in outlandish laps to sleep,
rock themselves like heavenly queens,
like their own sweet babes beyond with wings.

Postcard: Comics

The SCREEEEEE of a bagpipe's soundplay
shudders a lake
with inked lines and the foregone conclusions
sound effects. An amiable monster will rise.

Words
leap from our mouths, typed and rising
in bubbles, the cornered puff
kisses for readers:

What can we do, Uncle Mickey?

      It's plain I would freeze for you.

Run to the house!

      Grackles are pacing
      the front yard.

Let's go!

      You *must* tell me more,
      love, do you see?

We're in luck!
Here's a trapdoor!

Wheeeee!

Appetizer, for You

Chow chow
is a common German pickle,
a random mix of August, corn,
and spice: the taste is plain,
as plain as life; the feel
upon the tongue is fancy,
fickle.

Rally

The Delta Ohio CycleRama just broke up a whole
hot afternoon, with Crazy Ed of course
leading the 200, Sunday spun behind him like braids.

I was out front in my striped green plastic
lounge chair, propped and dull.
I was thinking I had them, and I might have

had Kid Korman pulled in, gravel hailing the hedge,
swung himself out of an ongoing cloud,
and walked my way through the chicory stalks, mildly
asking lady got some gas (form-a-gasket, band-aid),
and I'd have said, take off your helmet sweetface
let me see your hair. Bright Baby Blue and Sugar Sal
I would have asked in, admired the gloves, boots, glitter
crashgear, and led them into shade and set out ice
and green mint tea in fine glasses
and said, sweets we must do this more often.

The Light Has Changed

Now that the mornings rise
golden against the roof, what have I done
with the many-shaded darknesses
I used to roll and roll, smooth in my palms?

The light has changed.
I hear warblers spinning
tree through tree and now I believe
I will go beyond belief and be wind-drawn.

Listen. You shift in your sleep.
I have wanted to be the owl
woman determining dusk. My eyes
see the small black cats asleep.

Night is no longer my dark
and days twirl like leaves.
I have nothing. But watch
how I drift skyward

silently winged, feathered as if at your touch
the folds of wavering curtains drew back.
I sweep over acres of stubble, then
settle in elm, unshadowed.

The End of March

The darknesses as we talk
gather towards love, simply,

follow the narrowing lengths
like the run of limb

through the same spring rained on
fruitfulness of maple fringe

tips, the red puffed
filled ones. Tap that tree.

Disclaimer

I never said July would be good to us,
not with the long wheat field torn down
and the Funk's G corn skyrocketing—
nothing goes easy through those heaves.
And one day, one of the immaculate
in-the-beginning days, with the sun
plated high and hammered clear as a wish,
I walked where I once imagined walking,
past the barn, nettles, bromegrass, and on
through alfalfa, and the next alfalfa field,
across a fence of poison ivy into woods
where the swarmed mosquitoes took me
like the blank larval body ants carry
unceremoniously to their own place.

In the middle of the heat of a July woods
it is impossible to see through the brush to the stream,
it is impossible to recall the day of the week,
to define "vacancy," it is impossible
to disappear, to walk farther in, to keep what is not
within, like blood drawn, without fail.

Recurrent

What I have lost in the calm
drifted summer that drew us
in waves, into ourselves,
I am coming to understand.

I told you before of the time
in the Atlantic I thought I would swim
with the jeweled eyes of fish
forever, but I rolled like a baby
back into fields of air.

I may not have said
how with pulses and tides I brood,
thinking salt, salt. Recalcitrant,
I dislike that twist of tongue—the taste
of yours was another,

freshwater, new. I remember saying
I could not leave you.
There could be no reason.

And it's true I never was careless
at the shore as a child,
not with the sand carving its sea-going
spaces under my feet.

Like War

Voiceless
as lizards, the ragged-backed
desert lizards, sand tongues
gliding—we are not easy to name,
not easy to find.
If we move, a landscape shudders,
no more.
The slight dust returns
as itself in gravel; air
continues its drift
ocean to ocean.
We are bodies—
that we know.
We have loved each other
more than the houses who stand near
one another, more than the cities
linked ecstatically.
We with reptilian thighs
have loved each other more than lists,
more than names, or tests.
More than pools.
Still there is silence
everywhere like the cover of stippled camouflage
evolved with a fear
that momently living bodies
loving
were no defense.

Driving

In October rains, frogs out of ditches
fly to a hundred deaths on Wetherby Road.
They are silver and smooth-bellied.
Once my car skidded in the slick
through dark and familiar swamp.

Then again in spring, the warm mornings,
ordinary turtles set out,
crossing the same places and cracking
firm and complete against tread.

I head down the road at these times
through their flood, their amphibious planet,
while nerves in my wrists and ankles
pulse, hold the wheel, ride the throttle,
the clutch. I will get through this place,
drive straight home, no trouble.

Elegy

Pithless, the woody stem
like bamboo
whistles, and sheep knee-deep
beyond the hill in hay
slightly
turn their heads, blink
aimlessly.

Hollowness
fills a ghost,
channels the morning
wind into cries.
A flute cannot sing for joy.
Pipes of the lungs take in,
give out numbed songs.

In the house, termites blind
as corpuscles
eat through cellulose
binder, structure.
And the body of tree,
limb, plank,
trunk veined—

what had been
core and safe
writhes with strangers.
The heart sifts through a season,

finds no consolation
that all dust
in another millenium
presses toward rock—

the bone, the horn, the subterranean heap
of emptied cells,
tunnelled walls, the wooden
flutes of spent song.

December: Drying Corn

Two-story bins whirl through the night;
inside, yellow grains collide in their shriveling,
plummet through fanned winds
like rolls of a universe;
propane thrums, and the sweet roasted
yum yum galaxies crackle.

Into the night unwinds a scented wilderness
unimagined by sure-fire grandfathers,
unknown to the first women threshing seeds.

Now it is possible without myth
to burn and to burn and to drive off steam
all night in its agèd curls,
into the dawn light with the foam of an ocean.

The marvels of weather a farmer stirs
in a bucket, a barrel of new riddles:
with a handy, immediate magic
white smoke vaporizes the last

and most hidden drops in a kernel.
Like annointing oils, they hit the fire,
snap with a small click of tongue, and are gone.

It is, after all, the old rule, new run:
what's dry will keep. Dry; mummify; not die.

I have not told my neighbor I fear for his life,
lighting the fire at dusk. Its roar
drives over fields, vibrates through houses,
behind the TV flickering. Past midnight
when he checks the moisture and cuts the gas,
in the silence, the silence fallen in curtains,
I can tell that he takes a handful of corn,
rattles it like dice, then brushes his dry cheek
for comfort, with the back of his hand.

He walks to his house like a specter,
another traveler through the dry winds of space.